THE END OF THE ROAD

Marcia,

"... everyone wants to live on the mountain, but all the happiness and growth occurs while you're climbing it." — Andy Rooney

Thank you for your friendship!

Priscillamae

PRISCILLAMAE OLSON

THE END OF THE ROAD
Full Circle Home

TATE PUBLISHING
AND ENTERPRISES, LLC

The End of the Road
Copyright © 2015 by Priscillamae Olson. All rights reserved.

No part of this publication may be reproduced, stored in a retrieval system or transmitted in any way by any means, electronic, mechanical, photocopy, recording or otherwise without the prior permission of the author except as provided by USA copyright law.

This book is designed to provide accurate and authoritative information with regard to the subject matter covered. This information is given with the understanding that neither the author nor Tate Publishing, LLC is engaged in rendering legal, professional advice. Since the details of your situation are fact dependent, you should additionally seek the services of a competent professional.

The opinions expressed by the author are not necessarily those of Tate Publishing, LLC.

Published by Tate Publishing & Enterprises, LLC
127 E. Trade Center Terrace | Mustang, Oklahoma 73064 USA
1.888.361.9473 | www.tatepublishing.com

Tate Publishing is committed to excellence in the publishing industry. The company reflects the philosophy established by the founders, based on Psalm 68:11,
"The Lord gave the word and great was the company of those who published it."

Book design copyright © 2015 by Tate Publishing, LLC. All rights reserved.
Cover design by Nino Carlo Suico
Interior design by Jomar Ouano

Published in the United States of America

ISBN: 978-1-68097-386-0
Biography & Autobiography / Personal Memoirs
15.05.29

This book is dedicated to my parents,
Laura and Forrest
Mewhorter.

Contents

1	A Passport to Adventure	9
2	The Old Country School	13
3	Impact of Poverty	21
4	Resourcefulness and Versatility	25
5	Electricity Comes to Tuckaway	35
6	Taking the Grandchildren Home	39
7	The Last Sunset	43
8	Laughter Is the Best Medicine	47
9	Kaleidoscopic Impressions	55
10	A Coincidence You Say?	63

1

A Passport to Adventure

> All our actions take their hue from
> the complexion of the heart.
>
> —William Thompson Bacon

The car horns honked and bleated as streams of cars traveled south from Eau Claire, Wisconsin down Highway 10 toward the little town of Mondovi. Their resounding horns announced the end of World War II. I was just nine years of age, but I remember the day like it was yesterday.

My first recollection, or encounter, with Tuckaway Farm was during that summer of 1945. One bright promising morning, Mom appeared dressed in a long-sleeved shirt, coveralls, and straw hat drawn tight under her chin and directed me to dress the same.

She hitched the horse to our buggy, and we headed out. Our destination was unknown to me. I can still see the little white house tucked way back between green woods and hills as we rounded the high curve on County B. It appeared almost magical, nestled among hill and forest, tickling my senses and setting my imagination free. I really didn't have to imagine such a place because it really existed right before my very eyes.

The horse clipped along at a merry gait and seemed anxious to learn its destination and the reason for our adventure. As was I. In due time, we turned into what became a one-half mile, narrow dirt road giving us time and the option of sitting back to enjoy the abundance of peaceful natural beauty.

Hidden in the valley was a quaint, antiquated, well-worn house mirrored by an equally aged woodshed, garage, cream house, and barn. We had discovered the charm of an old farmstead in the midst of orchard and undomesticated grasses overgrown on one side, answered by hills and trees all around on the others. It made me want to reach for the clouds and soak up the sunlight as it warmed my face. Was this something personal or an experience that would happen to every traveler that ventured into its treasure-trove presence? Had we perhaps discovered a high road to adventure? Was this a passport to a summer's excitement?

An elderly lady occupied the house. She too was clad in long shirt and overalls when she came out to meet and greet us. She offered us a cool drink in the shade of a monstrous oak tree that stood near a quaint root cellar.

I was initiated into the sorority of berry pickers that day. You would have laughed to have seen this small army heading into the thick woods on its quest for blackberries, blackcaps, and red-fruited raspberries. Each of us tied the legs of our overalls legs with binder twine to hold the hems down when they tangled with bushes and briars. Around each of our waists, we had a big belt with the handle of a milk pail in its grasp so that our hands were free to pick berries.

I had never seen any kind of berry picking in the wild before. Nor had I ever trudged in thick trailing brambles of berry bushes that seemingly had claws and thorny tentacles to tackle me. I was in for a tough day's work. We had to literally fight our way through the berry bushes, but our pails filled quickly with the juicy inch-long blackberries. I ate and picked and picked and ate and trudged out of the woods with a stained face.

I quickly fell in love with this little old farm tucked securely back in the hills that harbored luscious wild berries free for the just the picking. I don't remember much about the four-mile trek home, nor for that matter the trip out the one-half mile long driveway back to County B. Happy, tired, but contented, my eyelids grew helplessly heavy. In fact, it seemed like it all had to have been a wonderful dream.

Mom and the faithful mare found the way home just fine along the country road. Before I even knew it, we were at our tiny rented house on Highway 37. I held the horse while Mom unloaded the many pails of berries onto the porch, and then she unharnessed the horse and set her free. But our work had just begun as there were berries to pick over and then process in the pressure cooker.

That was the only berry-picking adventure we had that summer, but Mom had been transfixed with that little farm cradled by the hills and woods. It would be about three years later that Mom would make an offer to buy what she termed Tuckaway Farm.

Some people say that home is just wherever the heart is, but it was living at Tuckaway Farm that brought stability to our lives and offered the really first opportunity to put down roots and to possess a genuine sense of having a home.

2

The Old Country School

> Favorite people, favorite places, favorite memories of the past…These are the joys of a lifetime…These are the things that last.
>
> —Unknown

Three and one-half miles uphill and down from Tuckaway Farm was a two-room white country school with blue shingle roof. It sat on a small plot of land amid farmers' fields at the corner of Highway 10 and County B. Actually, it was a three-room building as there was a small and narrow kitchen squeezed in between the primary and intermediate grade rooms. There were two teachers. One taught grades 1 through 4, and the other taught grades 5 through 8.

It had a big cast iron pot-bellied stove in each of the two classrooms. Each of us students took turns carrying in wood, but only the teachers would stoke each of the fires. They would bank them well, so they only needed to stop teaching infrequently to put in more wood to keep us all warm.

At recess, we'd sometimes put on a record and square dance if there was inclement weather. Then when the temperature was warm, we would vigorously play softball. Sometimes, we would practice on the high jump that was made with a bamboo fishing pole lodged on nails at varying heights on two posts. If we were unable to scale the height, the bamboo pole would drop off the nail.

Also in nice weather, children would be on their knees around a circle drawn on the sandy ground. Each would hold a large glass marble called a shooter. Each child would have a bag of smaller marbles. The game of marbles is kind of like playing pool by using one's fingers as a pool stick. The middle finger and thumb were used to propel the shooter marble that would then hit a smaller marble toward a predetermined goal.

Someone once wrote that, "In the cookies of life, friends are the chocolate chips." Recess was a great time to form bonds of friendships. We played a lot of large group games and tried to include everyone. One game we played was called Red Rover. One student who was "it" went to the center of the yard. The rest of us spread out in one long line across the yard. The student in the center would call out, "Red Rover, Red Rover, won't you please come over?" All of us would scramble and run at one time to the other side trying not to be caught. If we were caught, we had to stand in the center also and try to catch other students. Before long, so many people had been caught that it was progressively harder to escape being caught.

We used a volleyball, or on occasion a softball, to play a game called Annie Annie Over. Half of my classmates would go to one side of the building, and the other half would go to the opposite side of the school building. We would all call in chorus, "Annie Annie over," as one person threw the ball over the roof. If the ball did not go over, we'd call, "Pig's tail." Everyone on the other side waited eagerly to see if the ball would come near them so that they could catch it. Once the ball did successfully come over, that side would then call out in unison, "Annie Annie over."

After the first snowfall, one of the older kids who finished his or her work first would be sent out ahead of everyone else to make a very large circle across the school yard. He or she would have to tramp the snow down by circling around and around. Once the circle was plainly stamped down, the student would cut through the circle as though cutting a pie into eight pieces. At the very middle of the pie, another very small circle was tramped down. This very little circle was the "safety zone." Now the yard was prepared for the entire grades to play Fox and Geese. All of us donned snowsuits, scarves, caps, mittens, and boots eager to escape the fox. We all became imaginary geese and ran from the fox's grasp. The safety zone held only six to eight kids, so we were quickly pushed out by others scrambling to safety. Before long, the fox had a lovely flock of geese for his dinner.

On days when the snow was new, soft, and piling deeply, we loved to play Angels in the Snow. We'd lie down and wave our arms and stretch our legs wide and then pull them in and click our heels. Imagine—children's angels all over the school yard. If an alien ship passed over, no doubt the beings aboard would be afraid to land. We'd all resemble snowmen as we scrambled back into the warmth of the cloakroom to remove our outer wear.

One of our favorite group games was Dodge Ball. We all stood in a circle, joined hands, and then stepped three steps back. The classmate who was "it" stood in the middle and threw a soft volleyball at us. We tried to dodge the ball, but if we were hit, we were out.

In the spring, boys often wanted to play baseball and the girls softball. Both essentially have the same rules. Even our teachers got involved as the umpire and scorekeeper. We oftentimes played on two diamonds so everyone could be actively involved. We were excited to complete our schoolwork so we could go out to recess. When our school would travel and compete with another school, it is no secret that the teachers liked to talk. They would get absorbed in their conversation and lose track of the actual score, thus cheating one school or the other out of their due. Since it was a big deal to us kids, we have long remembered when our side was miscalculated.

On a bright sunshiny day, we sometimes played Shadow Tag. Someone would be "it" and attempt to run and step on our shadows. If we could not turn fast enough to cast our shadows in a different direction, we would have to become "it" and pounce on someone else's shadow to get a reprieve and catch our breath.

Each spring and fall, our school would compete with another country school in what we called a Field Day. There always were softball games, high jump, races, ball throws, hurdles, broad jump, jacks, and marbles. What we didn't realize was that we were exercising large and small muscles that counted as our physical education requirements because we had no school gym. Most of us had to do farm chores at home, too, so no one needed to worry about enough exercise, I guess.

One time, we had a basket social. We girls fixed a nice lunch and placed it in a pretty decorated box. Our names would be tucked inside the boxes. No one was supposed to know whose box was whose, but if we girls had a favorite boy as a special friend, we sneaked him the pertinent information. After a boy bought a girl's lunch, the boy and girl sat in the same desk seat to eat.

Almost every Friday, we had a spell down. All the kids, grades 5 through 8, would stand up in two lines. Each of us would be given a word to spell. We would have to sit down if we misspelled the word. One time, every one of us, but one, went down on the word *vacuum*. Out came the dictionaries.

I suppose you have seen the typical school desks used in country schools, but did you know that some were all attached together in a row? Some of us for whom the love bug had bitten found them to be very convenient for hand holding. The boy or girl in front would let his or her hand drop under the seat, while the girl or boy behind would just lean forward with one elbow on the desk and the other on their knee and extend a hand forward to meet their friend's hand. It also proved to be a handy seating system to pass notes during class without the teacher noticing.

"Don't forget to check this week's duty list," our teacher prompted us each Monday morning. Wow, it was such an honor to discover my own name beside a task assigned to me. Can you imagine being tickled pink for the honor of working? And work we did. Our jobs had to be done in rain, sunshine, snow, or cold weather. And Wisconsin's winters can get very cold!

Pumping water at the outdoor pump and carrying pailful after pailful can be quite physically challenging. You see, we carried water for both classrooms and for the cook in the little kitchen too. She required many pails full of water just to do the dishes.

To be assigned in cleaning the outdoor latrine, or "john" as we affectionately called the outdoor toilet, gave the least status. The boys' and the girls' bathrooms had to be swept, and toilet paper supplied daily. All the time, the door would be braced open, and the lid closed to reduce the stench of the sharp-smelling, acrid odor. Occasionally, a school board member would drop shovels full of lime down the holes to pacify the pungent smell.

One of us would be appointed to sweep the floor of the classroom, cloak hall, and porch. Inspection followed each task, so our very best effort was required.

The job of choice was caring for the many blackboards because then for a few minutes, we could pretend to be the teacher. First, the huge black slates had to be erased. Then the felt erasers were gingerly carried out of doors so as to not get chalk on a freshly swept floor. *Clap, clap, clap.* Erasers were socked up against each other. Chalk dust filled our lungs. It was such self-important work.

Bringing in the wood, armful after armful, for both classrooms and the kitchen was a very heavy and hard job. It was usually assigned to the biggest and strongest classmates. During the winter, the old pot-bellied cast iron stove seemingly gulped down one stick of wood after another. It was like a big fire-mouthed dragon devouring its prey. It was always hungry. The bigger kids also had to carry buckets of burned out ashes and pour them into a pile out of doors.

Washing the desk tops and seat benches required only a once-a-week effort. However, that student was also required to dust the classroom daily.

Someone would always have to walk around the playgrounds to ensure that all balls and equipment had been brought into the building for the night. Rain, dew, and snow could wreck gear if left out in the elements.

It was a joy to be chosen as the cook's helper. The cook prepared the meal, but she needed help at the last minute to serve the food. Smaller children also needed assistance to pick up and balance a napkin, silverware, milk, and plate of hot food while walking back to a desk without spilling.

Seldom were we ever assigned homework. Our teachers knew that farm work immediately awaited our arrival home after school. Many of us got up to chores, then school, and then chores again. We always felt needed and an important part of the family. We took pride in doing our jobs indoors and outdoors. Our work was our play. We really were little adults.

At Christmastime, we'd all have decorations to make, pieces to learn to recite, songs to sing, and plays to act in. We'd practice for weeks. Excitement would build until we'd nearly explode before the night of the program would finally arrive. Parents and neighbors would crowd the walls of our little classroom. Most families had several miles to travel to reach the school—some having come by car, while some by horse and wagon, and horse and buggy. The program was a really big deal for the students and something for the whole community to look forward to. After the program, Santa would enter with his bag of fruit and nuts. The room would be abuzz with everyone whispering a guess as to who the Jolly Old Man was for that year. Everyone would enjoy a hearty visit over a lunch that seemingly only farm women know how to prepare.

In the summer, the schoolhouse would be used to teach Bible school for all ages. It was a great opportunity to see friends not seen since the close of the school year. In addition, our school was used for 4–H Club meetings once a month. The 4-H program played an instrumental part in my late preteen and beginning teenage years.

My mother had taught me so many domesticated skills. Also, I had worked side by side in cucumber, bean, and large cabbage fields qualifying me to participate in 4-H club. The produce was sold to local stores, a canning factory, and from the back of a trailer along Highway 37, or in the Eau Claire Farmers' Store lot.

Belonging to 4-H afforded social outlets. We had softball games to participate in or to cheer on. Achievements were earned by giving demonstrations to the other members of the club of how to do or make something. Once a year, the entire 4-H club had the opportunity to visit each other's home to see close up and personal the projects and products accomplished during that current year.

In addition, each member had the opportunity to take various products to the county fair. I had entries in sewing, embroidering, baking, canning, gardening, and dairy. There were dress reviews to model articles of clothing sewed. Interspersed were essay contests and speeches to enhance and impact my life.

However, it took my mother to mentor and patiently teach me. How grateful I am today for my mother's patient lessons and for my willingness to have learned the various skills.

Finally, the eighth grade state exam would be taken, and if successfully completed, the day for graduation would arrive. We eighth graders left the little country school for Mondovi High School as big ninth graders come the fall.

3

Impact of Poverty

> In the quiet, the heart finds voice to speak. In the
> speaking, the soul finds cause to sing.
>
> —Unknown

In my earliest years, Christmases generally came and went with no gifts. My parents had lost their farm and everything they owned but the shirt on their backs, during the Depression era. We were dirt poor.

My dad had had only a fourth-grade education after his father's early death. Without an education, it was doubly hard to find work. He became a sharecropper, or farmed on shares, in default. Our family moved frequently where work and housing could be found. On one occasion, we were homeless. We found shelter in a ramshackled, abandoned house on a friend's property. On its door was posted a sign stating the house was condemned and not fit for human occupation. I still remember my tall father putting his arm high up on the doorframe, and I was watching his body shake, wracked with heart-wrenching groans and uncontrollable sobbing as he tore the sign down. Quite soon, we'd be on the road again having to start over at yet another school.

One Christmas, we kids each were thrilled to get an apple and an orange from the man who owned the farm my father was share-farming. Another Christmas season, when I was about five, my daddy discovered a unique Christmas gift for me in a granary attic. It was a doll house. He arranged with the farmer to borrow it for one week so that I could play with it. My seven-year-old brother's Christmas gift was to take scraps of cloth and sew curtains for the doll house.

What would you have played with when there were no toys or games? What would you have read when there were no books, magazines, or newspapers? Certainly, there were no DVDs, CDs, movies, television, cell phones, computers, iPads, or other modern-day video games.

Would you have liked to brush your teeth with soda and salt? How about washing your face and shampooing your hair with soap made from lard?

Would you feel okay about getting one stick of gum as your only allowance for a week's work well done?

Eli Khamarrow put poverty into words, "Poverty is like punishment for a crime you didn't commit." There were incidents of public disgrace and being blamed for things because of the perception that my family lived on the other side of the tracks. I learned that false rumors and abuse, rather words or actions, do hurt. In addition, I learned that bullies and dishonest people come in all sizes, shapes, ages, professions, and even in persons of authority.

Similarly, I learned that forgiveness is a long journey, and that it has the power to release me from anger. It allows me to receive the healing that I need. Forgiveness builds the foundation to experience strength, faith, courage, hope, direction, joy, love, and peace during life's challenges. The consequence and end result of an unforgiving and festering heart stand in the way of becoming all that God created me to be. I also learned that I do not have to bear the burden to be the judge, because Judgment Day is of a certainty.

One lesson I learned was that my happiness was not dependent upon what I had, but my happiness was found in my faith and in what I learned in the work that was expected of me for the good of my entire family. Happiness came with a sense of being needed and skilled and productive. Happiness was in giving of myself in work, not in getting possessions. Happiness was in knowing I was loved and needed and in being taught to be competent in so many areas. Mom had taught me to cook, bake, garden, can, preserve both produce and meats, sew, and embroidery. I had no earthly possessions, but I developed an inner strength and genuine happiness. Happiness was in acknowledging the reality of today, setting goals and envisioning dreams for a brighter future.

It's true that I experienced insecurity, as well as social, environmental, and educational deprivation. However, life dramatically changed for me when my family moved to the little farm at the end of the road.

4

Resourcefulness and Versatility

> A rich child often sits in a poor mother's lap.
> —Danish Proverb

My mother is my unsung hero. Among many other talents, she was a creative seamstress. Mom's old treadle sewing machine was simply magical. She sewed far into the night, oftentimes singing as she sewed. My favorite dress was of multiple yellow fabrics—a piece from this hand-me-down and a piece from that hand-me-down creatively sewn together into a "yellowish" dress my size and to my liking. However, nothing could compare to my jacket.

My prized jacket was constructed from several different items of clothing. It was wool and lined warm against the winter's cold. Pieces of solid and plaid greens, blacks, and grays made up the jacket. There were set-in pockets and the most beautiful buttons that were foraged from donated articles of clothing. I was so proud to wear Mom's latest and wonderful creation. She made it with love just for me.

Wouldn't you be frustrated if you had to sew clothes for yourself or your children and almost never be able to afford to buy yardage of fabric?

Mom never let our poverty defeat her. Handoffs were taken in at the seams, or seams let out, or a piece added. Sometimes she used flour sacks for a blouse or a skirt, but flour sacks were generally sewed together to make sheets for our beds.

Frequently, Mom would gingerly take apart a donated article of clothing. Then without the luxury of having a pattern, she'd "eyeball" and cut out a new dress, or blouse, or slacks. Well, not not new, but new to us, as we had never worn the article of clothing before.

I was fourteen or fifteen years old before I ever had a store-bought article of clothing. I bought my first long winter coat with money I had earned helping to harvest and sell one-half acre of cabbage. My only other purchase was a mattress to sleep on.

My grandmother used to tell me that my mom's wonderful noodle recipe was really a hand-me-down. She said that when she was growing up, her family used to have a large black cauldron hung on a tripod over a fire in the yard. Noodles would be added throughout the day as needed to feed large numbers. It would be a perpetual pot never running dry.

Her family traveled by covered wagon early on in her life, so for weddings and funerals, the extended family would come and spend several days. I am even told that the night that my parents were married, guests had to stay overnight at Grandma's house because the train was snowed in, and everything had come to a halt. Guess what was on the menu?

I kid you not, my mom made the most delicious chicken and noodles anyone could ever wish to eat. She handed the recipe down to me, and I have handed it down to my daughter. My mom became synonymous with chicken and noodles. Just ask anyone who has ever had the special privilege of placing their feet under her table.

Maybe you'd like to make homemade chicken noodles. You'll need three well-beaten eggs, nine tablespoons of milk, a healthy pinch of baking powder and salt, plus enough flour to make a dough just stiff enough as not to be sticky to the touch.

Pour out the dough onto a heavily floured board and knead. Roll out to a pie crust's thinness. Lightly flour the surface of the rolled out dough. Then roll up. Cut the roll into thin segments of a noodle's width. Gently toss the noodles into boiling chicken broth from which the boiled chicken has been removed and ready to be fried. Cook the noodles uncovered for the first ten minutes, and then cook them covered for another ten minutes. If desired, add grated carrots, minced onion, and chopped celery for greater flavor. If more liquid is needed, add more water and a bouillon cube to the pot.

You might think that if my family lived on a small farm that there wouldn't be times when we would have little food to eat. However, you would be wrong. My mother and I would can seemingly hundreds of jars of fruits and vegetables during the summer. My father and brother butchered pork, beef, and poultry to provide meat. In addition to meat that Mom and I canned, we wrapped meat in meal-sized packages and placed the packages in huge crocks and then nestled them into the deep snow in our back yard during the winter.

Even with hard work and careful planning, these specially preserved foods would eventually run out before the winter's end and the summer's new crops.

Some weeks, we were out of available food and groceries, but we were not actually hungry. Mom took our cows' milk, the hens' eggs, and the rationed canned fruit and whipped all of them up together. She then put the mixture into the pail of the ice cream maker. She added a mixture of salt and snow, all the while turning the crank, which twirled the ice cream pail around and around until the mixture congealed into yummy ice cream.

Mom made those weeks of stretching the money memorable and adventuresome. Every night, she added a different type of canned fruit to that night's ice cream. While eating ice cream as the main diet for a week might sound impossible, I looked forward to guessing what flavor Mom would have each night and also who would get to lick the dasher. At Christmas, Mom would fold in chips of a cinnamon stick to make it special.

I realize now that when my brother and I hunted rabbits and squirrels that it was serious business and not a sport. My mother would soak the skinned animals in soda water overnight to remove the wild taste before frying or baking them. Fried rabbit and squirrel were so good, but Mom's baked rabbit in white sauce was delectable.

Today, you can buy rabbit in the store. Maybe you'd like to try this recipe. Cut dressed rabbit or squirrel into serving pieces by disjointing legs at the body and joints. Split down the center back and through the breast, cutting each half in two. Dip meat in melted butter, and then into flour or crushed corn flakes or corn meal. Brown in hot fat and then reduce heat and cook slowly about one hour.

One day, my lunch consisted of only pickled apples. It was the only thing that my Mother had available for her to send in my lunch.

Today, most people like to have Ragu spaghetti sauce, or another brand, for pasta dishes. In those days, it was a struggle to buy just one can of regular Campbell's tomato soup that had to stretch for feeding seven mouths if having soup for supper, or if serving a small package of macaroni. Sometimes the macaroni had to be eaten plain. I don't remember that any of us complained. We all did our best to do our jobs at home and at school. We were self-disciplined and needed few reminders.

If Mom had sour milk, she would boil it on the kitchen's large range stove in a huge kettle. After the sour milk bubbled and boiled thoroughly, white chunks of cottage cheese would appear in a thin semi-bluish liquid. Mom would use the dishtowel sieve to catch the pieces of cottage cheese, while the liquid, or whey, was either used in homemade bread being baked that day, or as slop for the pigs.

We would harvest cabbage from our cabbage patch. After washing it thoroughly for dirt and cabbage worms, we'd shred it. Then the shredded cabbage was layered with salt in a big crock in the root cellar and allowed to ferment to make sauerkraut.

We'd harvest the carrots and the potatoes from our garden and then bury them in a mound of sand in the root cellar to preserve them for eating months later.

Mom knew how to stretch the meal ticket. When we butchered, no part of the animal was wasted. Mom even processed head cheese and tongue. The liver and heart were also utilized. Cooking lard, as well as soap, was made from the animal's fat. The tail made delicious soup stock.

As a farm child where butchering occurred annually, I was glad to be reassured that people occupied the highest position on the chain of life and therefore would never be eaten.

Churning Butter

Mom or one of us, more likely my brother, would milk the cows. Milk with high fat content from certain cows was put into a separator, and the thick cream would be saved out and cooled.

After washing the butter crock and the churn-dasher carefully, the rich thick cream was poured in. One of us kids would be assigned to push the dasher in, down, out, in, down, and out until our arms would nearly fall off. At every stroke, the cream was forcefully stirred and beaten. Eventually, tiny chunks of butter floating on the milk would appear.

The chunks of butter were caught in a cloth flour sack sieve, and the liquid called whey would drain through the homemade sieve into a clean bowl. This liquid was called buttermilk and either drunk, or used for baking. Salt was kneaded into the pieces of butter and then pushed hard into a mold.

Baking Bread

On one day every week, breads were made. We made loaf bread, cinnamon rolls, and dough-dads. I thought that a warm slice of bread was a delicious gift, or reward, for all the effort involved.

Yeast was dissolved in a cup of warm water with some sugar. The interaction of the sugar and yeast caused the bread to rise making the bread light and soft. Cinnamon rolls were made out of bread dough that had risen but had not yet been kneaded. The bread dough was dumped onto a floured board, and a rolling pin was used to roll and flatten the bread dough. Butter was spread across the top of the flattened bread dough. Cinnamon and sugar came next. Then the dough was tightly rolled up. A sharp knife was used to slice the rolled dough into inch-thick pieces. A clean dish towel was placed over the rolls to rise before being put into the oven.

Mom could make a special day where none existed. She would knead up her tremendous bread dough. My brother, being two years older than me, would mind the large kettle of hot fat. Mom instinctively knew the size her pinch of dough needed to be. She dropped each piece into the scalding fat. My brother would retrieve the browned dough-dads and drop each into sugar for the finished and yummy results. At Christmas, Mom made some chocolate to dip the dough-dads in. What a heavenly treat. I can taste them now.

What would you and your family do if sugar was rationed? When I was a very little girl, sugar, gas, and tires were rationed due to the World War II. Mom would put a little bit of sugar in a baby food jar for herself and each of us children. Dad would get a pint jar reserved for him.

Sugar or Sorghum?

During my years at Tuckaway Farm, my dad planted sorghum, and we made our own sugar. The plant when full grown looked similar to a field of Indian corn but with spikelets. Dad harvested the sorghum plants and took them to a mill. At the mill, a juice was squeezed out of the sorghum plants that resembled corn syrup. Mom boiled and boiled the juice, or syrup, and a dark, quite bitter sugar was the end result. We respected and never wasted this sugar, even though now white sugar no longer needed coupons distributed by the government to buy sugar because the war had ended.

Harvesting and Preserving Apples

Mom would secure dates on the calendar for apple picking. She would plan dates for making apple pies, apple butter, apple sauce, spiced apple pickles, and canned apple slices.

One day was for the picking. Ladders stretched up into the apple trees' limbs and boughs bearing the weight of the grown-ups. We younger children scrambled on the ground, culling the good from the bad. Rotten apples cannot be used for anything, but apples with blemishes can be made into apple sauce and apple butter. Even apples where worms have tunneled though can be used once the areas are cut off and discarded.

By lunch time, our backs, knees, arms, and legs ached from crawling, crouching, bending, stretching, and reaching. Mom and we girls prepared a quick lunch and then we all headed back to the orchard to complete the first step in squirreling away our winter's source of apple sauce, apple butter, pickles, and canned slices.

Before nightfall, all the apples picked from the trees were rolled into the big wash tubs to soak and later to be gently rubbed for a thorough cleansing. The apples we kids picked from the orchard floor were hand-cleaned to avoid further traumatizing the already bruised apples.

The next morning, an enormous stainless steel kettle was chosen to be used to make the apple sauce. Mom said that aluminum kettles, and other types of pans, make the sauce taste bitter, and the apple sauce stains the pans. We each carefully cut off the salvageable parts and peeled each piece. The pieces quickly filled the huge pot. Mom added the condiments and banked the fire in the old wood cook stove.

While the apples cooked and turned to a mush, Mom placed a dishtowel on the bottom of each of our cake pans. Then after she had filled each jar with hot water, she put the jars on the folded towel. When the cake pan could hold no more jars, Mom added enough hot water to fill the pan three-fourth inch from the top. She put the pan of jars on the stove to heat. She explained that in this way, the jars from the basement would be disinfected. In another smaller pan of water, Mom put the jar lids and covers on the stove to also sterilize. Mom boiled a funnel cone and a measuring cup to have in readiness.

When the apple sauce had boiled and was a thick mush, a funnel was placed at the top of a sterilized jar. About three and three-fourth cups of sauce was needed to fill each quart jar. A clean cloth was used to quickly clean off any spilled sauce. Then a jar lid and cover were put on, and the cover tightened. All the completed jars were put on warm towels away from any draft. Throughout the evening, we'd have fun listening for a popping sound and keeping track of how many pops we heard. Mom said that those pops were music to a cook's ears because the pop meant that the jar had sealed, and her work was not in vain.

Early the next morning, Mom tenderly hand washed the outside of each jar, and we kids were told to carefully carry each jar to a shelf in the basement.

The next day was apple butter day. Again, we cleaned and boiled the jars, lids, and covers. We cut and saved only the usable pieces from the washed apples that had been saved from the orchard's floor. Mom cooked the pieces in much the same way as when making apple sauce, but apple butter is much thicker than apple sauce and tastes much different. Apple butter is intended to be a spread much like a jam on toast, or a slice of bread. Sometimes apple butter and warm bread served as a delectable dessert.

When your mom wants to make apple pie for supper, she has choices. She can go to the grocery store and buy a ready-made pie in the freezer or bakery aisles. Or she can buy frozen pie shells from the frozen department and make pie with fresh apples already picked and available in the produce department.

We had no refrigerator in our home, nor a freezer. We had no money to purchase frozen pie crust, if it would have even existed in the 1930s and 1940s. Our apple pies took the long road from the orchard to our table.

You already know the best apples were picked and reserved for apple pies. After being picked, soaked, and wiped, they were pushed onto a handheld cranked apple corer gadget. The apple corer peeled, cored, and sliced the apples. The seeds were discarded with the core. Mom would pack the spotless hot fruit jars with the freshly cut apple slices all ready for canning. So when Mom, or I, baked a pie, it was quite an ordeal compared to today. A canned jar of apple slices was fetched from the basement. The jar was washed first and then opened. The contents were then poured into our homemade crust.

So you want pie a la mode? Wait a bit please, while we make some homemade ice cream.

If we had a bumper apple crop, some of the very best apples were cleaned and then dipped into a thin coating of wax before being individually wrapped in newspaper. They were stored in an upstairs bedroom over the winter. These apples were rationed out for eating apples, or for baked apples. Baked apples were a delicacy.

We had some crab apple trees that provided miniature-sized apples. We used these tiny apples to make pickled apples.

Larger apples could also be cored and sliced so that the slices remained in circles. The circles were packed in jars with a pickle brine. Usually, we would only use pickled apple slices for a special holiday treat served with holiday meats. Red cinnamon candy would be added to give color to the holiday table to spice up the holiday meal raising spirits.

5

Electricity Comes to Tuckaway

> A candle loses nothing of its light
> by lighting another candle.
>
> —Kelly

As a young child, I mostly grew up in homes without electricity. Generally, our lighting in the house was given off by an Aladdin lamp. It had a special mantle rather than a wick like those used in a regular kerosene lamp. We had to share the one Aladdin lamp and coordinate our activities to have light where it was needed. The mantle could break very easily, so we had to be very careful. The lamp's globe had to be washed every few days so that light could shine through the glass.

For milking the cows and other chores after dark, a lantern filled with kerosene was hung on the barn wall, or carried to and from the barn to illuminate the way.

I marvel now that we didn't catch the barn on fire using the kerosene lantern throwing down hay from the mow. Sometimes, we even slid down the chute with the lantern in hand after we'd thrown down the last forkful of hay.

Probably, you can imagine how our lives changed that summer when electric current came to Tuckaway Farm. Even though we could not afford the appliances and electrical gadgets needed, having electric light revolutionized our personal lives. We eventually did get a refrigerator. We even had a yard light high on a pole to illuminate our way to and from the barn and for the other chores that had to be done in the winter's early darkness.

To flip a switch and find light in a room was a mystical miracle, almost a religious experience. I dared to believe I could use this electrical juice to curl my hair, forgetting for a moment that one needs electrical devices to accomplish this feat. So I had the same old two choices in regard to curling my hair— I could either sleep on hard knots of hair wound around a rag and then tied up at the top or continue to use the kerosene lamp and the antique curling rod. My little sister Judy had naturally curly hair, and I envied the attention she received.

Mom would leave the chores and come in from the barn in time to stick the antiquated curling rod into the globe of the kerosene lamp to heat. Then one by one, she would form what I believed to be the perfect curl. How happy her selfless act made me, and it inspired my whole day.

Having electricity didn't change some things. We still heated wash water in huge boilers for the washboard tubs and for the hand wringer washing machine. We still carried cold water to the rinse tubs. We still heated water to fill the round aluminum wash tub that sat in front of the range's open oven door on Saturday night. It served as a bathtub, or should I say, our community tub. Mom always had the last bath. Can you imagine that?

The kitchen range and the living room stove still ate wood at an alarming rate. Trees had to be felled.

After the tree was cut down and "Timber" was yelled warning anyone near to be alert, my dad and brother would stand on either side of the tree holding the handle of a bucksaw, thrusting it back and forth to cut the tree log into big lengths, but small enough to load onto a sleigh. The work horses pulled the sleigh home into the farmyard.

The heavy lengths of logs were then cut into chunks of wood with a self-made motorized saw. Each chunk of wood was then split into small enough pieces to fit into the stoves. My father and brother would brace a foot against the chunk of wood and then raise the axe high and then come down with incredible force. The big chunk would split in half. Then each half would be split likewise and then probably once again, depending on the chunk's original size.

All the pieces had to be stacked neatly in the woodshed. It was very important to stack them just like Dad said to prevent the whole row from falling or being exposed to the elements. Each morning and evening, we kids carried armloads of wood into the house to be used for cooking, heating water, and keeping the house warm. Sometimes we'd work as a team so that one would load the outstretched arms of a brother or sister. We were always happy to witness a glimpse of the impending springtime after carrying all those hundreds of loads of wood. Spring would offer new possibilities, plus work needed doing.

Once the snow had cleared, we kids would race to the plot of ground that Dad fenced in up on the hill near the barn. This pet cemetery was sacred to us and to our children after us. It overlooked the farm yard. To one side was an apple orchard. Above it, the windmill reached into the blue heavens. Many funerals were conducted. Boxes were lovingly lined with pretty fabric scraps. The beloved and faithful pets were carefully and prayerfully buried. Each pet's spot was marked with a cross.

It was a sad day when Tuckaway Farm was sold and no longer remained in the family, negating access to the precious cemetery.

However, years later, adult grandchildren were briefly permitted by the new owner to walk up the treasured hill where their pets were also interred.

6

Taking the Grandchildren Home

> The little reed, bending to the force of the wind, soon
> stood upright again when the storm had passed over.
>
> —Aesop

When I was young, we had no lawnmower. Once or twice a year, my father took a few swipes around our farmyard with his big, field hay mower. The grasses in the yard would grow so tall. It was much like wading through a hay or grain field. For the duration of our stay at Tuckaway Farm, I felt the long grasses gave me a real sense of being at home, grounded in this vast universe.

As time rolled on and I had children of my own, I brought my toddlers home to see Grandpa and Grandma. My parents had repurchased Tuckaway Farm in their retirement, making it possible for me to let my children catch the verve, enthusiasm, and ecstasy that had captured my soul. Tucked away at the end of a long, very narrow, rugged, dirt road was the place I could call home.

Perhaps you are thinking that taking my children home was child's play. I think in a sense, you may be right. Childhood and its play, as well as possession of toys, had passed me by in many respects.

Climbing to the top of a big hill with my husband, Gordon, and my children, Maylin and Glenna, to fly kites proved to be as exhilarating and fulfilling to us two adults as it was to our two children.

Donning warm duds and clamping on cross country skis in winter's chill found us in high spirits as we started mid-hill. We actually managed to remain standing and flowed through Tuckaway's rich valley alive with new fallen snow. We arrived back to the warm kitchen for hot chocolate. Obviously cold but chock-full of excitement and contentment of child's play together on the hill.

Another Saturday would find us scooting-up together to fit onto two sleds and then joyously gliding down the snow-covered hills back toward the farmyard. We'd laugh and challenge each other's sled to dare to drift further ahead than the other.

Grandpa and Grandma loved to go to auctions to find a good deal. A little sleigh and a cart brought satisfaction, not only to themselves, but to their grandchildren and to their adult children home for the holiday. Grandpa gave the little pony-sized horses a good workout anytime the grandchildren visited, regardless of the season.

My husband loved to visit Tuckaway Farm too and tried to come with his family as often as possible. One summer, he had to remain behind at our St. Paul suburban home to work his shift at the post office. The children and I would be rejoined with Daddy on the weekend. In the meantime, we tented under sprawling oaks among fragrant roses, peonies, and lilacs that bordered the front yard. The children played in the sand and mud to their hearts' content.

However, one day they stopped mid-play and excitedly insisted that I write down all the words that came tumbling out in elated and fragmented diction. They didn't want Daddy to miss out on any of the fun. Then hand in hand, the two walked the one-half mile winding driveway along a peat field of towering corn stalks to the rural mail box to mail a letter home to Daddy.

Grandma and Grandpa seldom traveled, but the extended family was drawn to Tuckaway Farm. We sat around huge platters heaped high with cobs of corn from the field. For dessert, we'd have tasteful dishes of canned berries from Grandma's basement.

To this very day, I can still see visions of the mounds of homegrown mashed potatoes smothered in gravy, also chunks of meat that Grandma had canned during butchering week. Buttered carrots just dug up from the sand mound in the root cellar were eagerly devoured. Who could forget the large stuffed turkey with the crisp, crunchy chestnut brown epidermis?

Never will my children, nor I, forget my brother Dean's wonderful chicken barbeques served up at the old picnic table. In the quietness of my heart, I can still hear the distinct clear singing and yodeling of the Zobrist cousins, floating down from the very top of a surrounding hill. It was like evening vespers. We all sat there in the approaching chill of the night not moving, enveloped with the awe of the moment. It was as though Angela Morgan was there and had spoken in person, "I will hew great windows for my soul."

Without any prompting, the almost magical spirit of Tuckaway streamed from my children's toddler days through their teenage years, welding their souls to a sense of extended family, and being at one with the universe.

7

The Last Sunset

> Oh, I will think of things gone long ago
> and weave them to a song.
>
> —Euripides

Even after retirement, times still were always hard for my parents, and ready cash was nonexistent. They were never free to forget that they had lost absolutely everything of a monetary value in the Great Depression in the 1930s. No opportunity had availed itself to have earned an employer-sponsored retirement plan.

I was a Depression baby who added one more mouth to feed and another body to clothe. Even so, my parents viewed my birth and life as a blessing.

I am forever grateful for my brief few years at Tuckaway Farm. But it is said that all good things must come to an end. Mom and Dad tried to hold onto Tuckaway Farm with Mom and us kids doing the farming during the week and Dad working in the Twin Cities loading lumber onto railroad cars and then coming home on the weekend.

My mother sensed that the only way out of poverty was to have a good education. She craved it for her children, and she herself completed her GED at the age of seventy-three. Mom determined that we kids would have an education, and it was time for our family to move where jobs and education were available.

Tuckaway was sold on monthly payments to a good neighbor who had a young family. The farmer died during a medical emergency, leaving his wife and several little children without an income. After his death, his wife offered to resell Tuckaway Farm back to my parents. My parents took the farm back but allowed this widow to live there until her children were grown.

Mom spent many long hours on the streetcar as both she and Dad worked in mundane, low-paying jobs in the Cities. On the weekends however, they regrouped back at Tuckaway Farm. They had industriously converted a milk house into a very small weekend cabin. Thus, Tuckaway Farm was preserved as a home base for the family at large to continue to return to.

When the farmer's family had grown and the house was vacated, Mom and Dad moved back into it in their retirement years. Eventually, they sold it to my brother, who never actually took possession and resold it when his marriage dissolved. Along with the disintegration of his marriage came the termination of our beloved Tuckaway Farm family celebrations and the dispersing of the family clan. Our sun set for the last time over the mystical hills of Tuckaway Farm.

By the time I was twelve, my mother arranged for me to work for a neighbor for one dollar a day and to save it toward a college education. I baked, cooked, cleaned, and cared for children. At age fifteen, after we had moved to the Twin Cities, my mother obtained a job for me in a nursing home. Then at ages sixteen to eighteen, I worked as a nurse's aide at the same metropolitan hospital that my mother had gained employment.

My monies were earmarked for college, but it was my brother who was immediately in need of monies to complete his teacher's college. It was decided that I would loan Dean the money so he could finish his senior year, and then he would repay me my first year of college from the money he would earn in his first year of teaching.

One fall when I was seventeen, my parents asked to have a conference. I was told that they were unable to keep their present house in the Cities and would have to live in the basement of a relative's house. My sister, Judy, who was four years younger than me would be going with them. It was then that I was told how proud they were of me and that they were confident that I could make it on my own. My girlfriend's parents invited me to live at their house so that I could complete high school. The previous year, I had been working thirty hours a week at the hospital. My principal arranged my class schedule during my senior year so that I could be dismissed at noon and thereby increase my work hours to forty hours per week.

My fellow students and teachers must have agreed with my parents that I would be successful as they voted me the girl "Most Likely to Succeed" in the entire senior class. Later, it was further confirmation with my inclusion in "Who's Who in Minnesota," and "Who's Who in the Midwest," for my various achievements in the field of education.

Very early on, my mother had insisted that I inquire what was required for entry to college. At that time in our life, we had no stationery. She gave me a piece of a brown paper bag. Many years later, a college official showed me the brown paper bag's inquiry letter and shared his heartfelt congratulations for a job well done. I had graduated with distinction with a bachelor of science in education adorned with the magna cum laude colors. Then it was on to a master's degree.

I tell you these things to confirm for you, if you are struggling, that regardless of unfortunate circumstances of poverty and deprivation that you may have been born into, education, hard work, faith, love, and forgiveness can help you blossom into a happy, successful, meaningful, and richly fulfilling life.

8

Laughter Is the Best Medicine

> When our hearts go home, joy stands waiting to greet us.
>
> —*Unknown*

I suppose all families have little anecdotes that they look back on with fondness, and as you will see, mine is no exception. One of my farm tasks was to walk up into the hills and down into the valleys, or into the dark haunting beauty of the woods to bring the cows home for milking each late afternoon.

A couple of times, we children literally could not find the cows and would have to go home empty-handed. Thus, Dad attached a bell to a collar around the neck of a cow observed to be a natural leader in the herd.

That took care of the problem until one day, when the cows went deep, deep, deep into the bowels of the thick woods.

Deeper and deeper, we followed the sound of the bell with no cows within our sight. But to our amazement, there was something awaiting us, at least a six-foot-by-four-foot raised mound of dirt. Being partially Indian and having found relics before, we wanted to respect our ancestors and were thinking that the mound was a sacred Indian burial ground.

I ran home to get my uncle Ben who was visiting. His curiosity was piqued wondering if we'd really exposed a burial of a far different sort that would be of interest to the police. He grabbed a spade and hurried back up through the hills with me. The cow's bell helped guide us as we entered the now secretive, darkening, dense, almost impenetrable woods.

You can imagine my pride to show my uncle Ben our find because he was so proud to be an Indian.

We got near the mound, and he plunged in with his shovel to investigate a bit. He was attacked by seemingly thousands of ants. He went flying out of the woods and ran back to the farmhouse with ants in his pants.

Making Supper for Threshers

You could say that Mom was always home, except for this one exception, even though a crew of threshers was coming in from the fields expecting supper on the table. Men from neighboring farms united to help each other harvest their crops and then moved on to another farmer's fields of oats or corn.

Housewives at each farm provided either morning lunch, noon dinner, afternoon lunch, or supper depending on when the men were still harvesting the fields on their farm. My Mom was confident that I could handle the evening supper and left me with careful instructions. For dessert, I was to make my now infamous chocolate cake recipe. Therein lies a life-long problem.

There was a young man of muscle but backwoods brawn in the threshing crew that day. He took a fancy to me and my cake and repeatedly said so.

I blushed and giggled. He kept repeating, "This is good cake, Priscilla, and you don't have to laugh either," in his drawn out characteristic tone.

From that very day forward at any meal in which I prepared something especially tasty, my dad would give his hysterical rendition of, "This is good, Priscilla, and you don't have to laugh either." Now that Dad is gone, I miss his teasing and special expression of gratitude for a good meal.

The Lopsided Cake

Tuckaway Farm's front yard had flowers, flowering bushes, birds, and Tiger Lilies lining the driveway and trees. It was a piece of nature not daily experienced by those of us who had grown and moved into the Cities. Chicken cooked on the grill fast became everyone's favorite summertime fare.

It was Grandpa's birthday. I had volunteered to bring a decorated birthday cake. I had made a special new recipe—a frosted torte with numerous beautiful layers. For some reason, the layers of the cake had slid on our trip down to the farm, but not in unison. The cake, although delicious, was a flop artistically. My daughter, Glenna, aged three, was sensitive to my dismay and wanted to be helpful. She said, "Just tell them I made it, Mommy." Bless her sensitive caring heart.

Papa Bear Soup

There probably isn't any child who has ever visited Tuckaway Farm for breakfast that doesn't know about Papa Bear soup. Grandpa loved oatmeal and wanted everyone to share in his delicacy.

Standing by a pot of oatmeal on the stove, he would stir and growl, and growl and stir. Little eyes would be large as saucers and willing mouths would try the Papa Bear soup. However, sometimes, a bowl would need a little more growl of encouragement. Papa Bear soup became synonymous with Grandpa.

Only White Cows Go to Market

The men had retired to the living room as the women cleared the table, put away the leftovers, and washed the dishes. The men made plans to pull the wool over my sister-in-law's eyes. She was told that the herd of white cows she had seen on her trip to Tuckaway Farm were white because they were ripe and ready to go to market. She was told that all cows turn white when they are ready to be sold to the market. On cue, each guy who came through the door took up the joke and convincingly carried on the monkeyshine.

The Glass of Water

Mom was hanging the wash and watching the wrestling duo near the clothes line. She told my brother and my dad to stop, fearing they would hurt themselves. They continued on, each using his ultimate strength. They were neck to neck, and someone needed to stop the bout.

Mom began to literally beat the two of them with a wet pair of overalls. They wrestled on. Mom hollered and fought them with the wet bibs before fainting flat out on the ground.

The wrestling came to an abrupt halt. Dad told my brother to go and get Mom a glass of water. My brother did as he was told and handed Dad the glass of water. Dad knelt over my mom and then he drank the whole glass of water. Later, Dad sheepishly explained that Mom had fainted; and thus she couldn't benefit from the glass of water, but he sure could.

Where Are They?

My children and my brother's children played Hide and Seek in the old farm house. My children, being a few years younger, tried as hard as they could but never could find the secret passage. To this day, as adults, they never have figured out how their cousins, Russell and Randy, got from the attic to the root cellar without leaving the house. The mystery remains.

Streaking

My folks aged, retired, and returned from the Twin Cities area to their beloved Wisconsin farm looking toward many years of retirement. They added a bedroom on first floor, a basement, and a furnace. One could literally now go from the kitchen to the living room, to the bedroom, to the bathroom, and all the way back around, having come full circle.

Being located in a secluded, solitary area, Mom was a bit concerned and carefully locked the door each night. Mom loved to sew at night when she could concentrate and not be bothered. As her sewing machine whirred and hummed, Dad was up to some good-natured tomfoolery behind her back. Suddenly, she heard loud fast running footsteps. My dad was streaking naked. He was running full throttle open around the complete circle. Mom frantically screamed for Dad to come and help her because someone had broken into their house.

In Need of Driver's Training

As a very young girl, I had driven tractor in the fields. Also, I had driven horses to pull the hay up into the mow. As well, I had ridden horses to cultivate weeds from the crops. So why not learn to drive a car? Dad said to go ahead. "Take it down and around the circle." His tone of voice was both stern and filled with a twinkle. He had pre-guessed my demise. I could not navigate the complete circle and ran atop of a huge oak stump. There I sat. My dad stood laughing his head off.

A Call to the Veterinarian

Something was terribly wrong with the entire herd of cattle. While I was at school, Mom had frantically called the town's vet. We kids came home from school to find Mom with a long stick walking behind this cow and then that cow, herding them around and around in a confined area. The cows walked unsteadily and wanted to just lie down.

Mom hurriedly requested that we kids take her place so that she could rest. She had been walking them practically the entire day. The cows had gotten into the orchard. We had previously picked and canned all the good apples, but the cows had eaten the apples that had fallen from the trees and had rotted. The cows were legally drunk from apple cider according to the veterinarian.

In the Quagmire

A half-mile dirt road can seem to be an eternity in length during a spring's thaw. The winter's snow and ice give way to the sun's melting rays. Once what was quite a firm, earthen basis yields to slushy mud. A car's tires just mire down. The more the driver steps on the gas, the deeper the car digs into the quagmire.

One spring, Dad had at least three, but probably five, of his grandsons in his car as he fought to get the car in from the main road to the house. One of his grandbabies came up with what he felt was the best solution to end all of Grandpa's struggles. He recommended that Grandpa build a roof, or cover, all the way in from County B to the house. He explained then there would be no rain to cause any mud. The problem was thought solved in this preschooler's mind.

Snitching the Epidermis

It is well-known in our family who the champion turkey skin snitchers are. This tasteful deed has even passed on to some of the grandchildren. My sister-in-law Marge and I won the all-time honors one year during the holiday season. If only Grandma had just had us carve the turkey and quickly loaded the slices onto a platter in the pantry and brought it right out to a waiting table, our assignment would have been accomplished without any repercussions.

One year however, the turkey was done well ahead of the other savory foods and was taken from the oven and covered up so it would remain warm. Now and then, my sister-in-law and I just could not resist. We'd lift the cover ever so slightly and pull a piece of the mahogany, delectable skin off and eat it.

Wouldn't you know, to our dismay, Mom decided that this year of all years, she would carve the turkey at the table so all could enjoy the pleasant and nostalgic occasion. When the turkey was unveiled, it had been stripped of almost all its skin covering. Old Tom was practically naked.

9

Kaleidoscopic Impressions

> We should so live and labor in our time
> That what came to us as a seed,
> May go to the next generation as blossom,
> And what came to us as blossom, may go to them as fruit.
>
> —Henry Ward Beecher

Mom was a woman of faith. While we attended church when we could wherever we lived, we often were without transportation in my earliest youth.

One Sunday, Mom was determined that we would attend services. She did the morning milking and chores before coming in to ready herself and three of us little kids. Then, she hitched up the mare to the buggy, and we started out to Mondovi.

It doesn't matter that services and Sunday school were over by the time we arrived. Mom had modeled the importance of church attendance that day and clearly demonstrated the source of her resilience in dealing with all that life had thrown her way.

Even now, as an adult, I know that God is real and near to me. He continuously reveals himself to me in nature. Sometimes, it is Tuckaway Farm that reminds me of God's love as seen in nature.

As Seen Through a Window

Hushed quietness settles over
Woods and valley as
White crystalline flakes
Softly alight on blade and bough;
Let the peace of God rule in your hearts,
Prompting one's mind and soul.

Tranquil calmness reconciles the
Questioning and contentions as
Light milk-white precipitation
Quietly transforms one's countenance;
For He is our peace,
Quickening one's reflection and comprehension.

Restful, alabaster snowfalls
In ever larger flakes as
Pure glistening diamonds
Innocently gather and validate;
That in Me you might have peace,
Refreshing one's body and spirit.

Spring is seen as a time of renewal and of new beginnings; however, one must learn to savor the winter while awaiting earth's season of new birth.

Promises of Spring

This morning I awoke
To a woods of splendor
With boughs laden
With wet fallen snow.
Tips of pine trees
Bowed down in reverence;
Peace be still;
I heard your small voice.

Cardinals dressed in brightest red
Hovered at each feeder
While rabbits and squirrels
Burrowed in their nests.
The woods was quiet
Clothed in awe;
I will never leave thee;
And I felt your presence.

The late spring's sunlight
Broke forth as the morning
With its rich warm rays
Creating rivulets of water.
The red oaks opened their arms
Welcoming a returning flock;
I have plans to give you hope and a future;
I rejoiced in Your promise.

From a very young age, visits to Grandma's house were very special to my daughter, Glenna. She and Grandma shared a common bond and love of literacy. The place where their likes and dislikes met head-on was a distinct dislike for Grandma's mince meat and pumpkin pies. "Only ice cream for me, please, Grandma."

Grandma

Sometimes in this world of ours,
There are things we don't understand,
Like how hopes and dreams can be shattered,
By just the wave of a hand.

The moments we've shared together,
Are now memories of special times,
Memories dear to the heart, Grandma,
Bound lurking within my mind.

You've taught me how to live my life,
To strive toward my every goal,
To be creative, honest, and loving,
And to keep faith within my soul.

You've helped me to become well-rounded,
Encouraging me with each passing day,
Expressing your loving concern,
By not showing, but leading the way.

Your family is here with you
To be forever by your side,
We love you ever so dearly, Grandma,
And these feelings we cannot hide.

As I go to sleep tonight,
I'll say a prayer for you,
To my dearest, loving, Grandma,
I love you.

—Glenna J

Grandpa was fun and laughter when he put on his silly antics. Also, who could forget the sleigh and cart rides with Grandpa at the reins? Or his doling out the sugar cubes to feed the ponies?

Grandpa

Sometimes life's not what it seems
Just fond old memories and broken dreams
Feelings of love, confusion, and fear
A show of strength by withholding tears.

A family's love, concern, and care
Sorrow, frustration, and mounting despair
A look at death, with teary eyes
Unsaid words and uncovered lies.

The End of the Road

A rusted chair, a broken swing
Cherished memories, the songs we'd sing
A white rose, an eternal love
A strengthened faith from above.

At the table, an empty place
Remembrances of your smiling face
The times shared, the love that's grown
Within my heart, has found a home.

A tender touch with tired hands
Always encouraging without demands.
From you to me, the love's passed on
Living forever and ending in song.

—Glenna J.

Even though decades have come and gone, Tuckaway Farm continues to weave its spell as Glenna takes a walk down memory lane.

A Return to Tuckaway

I take a long walk down that sandy, winding road, that leads to a place called Tuckaway. A quaint little white farmhouse, trimmed with blue, filled with the warmth of family and abundant love. The smell of the wildflowers that line the road and follow the sidewalk, lead me to the front door. In the porch stand work boots covered with mud, jackets wet from the summer's rain. From the kitchen the smell of freshly brewed coffee, and homemade noodles on the stove. The breeze from the window is cool and refreshing. I can hear the horses whinny outside, and the cattle stir. The warmth of the kitchen surrounds me as I take in all my senses will allow. The table is set. The TV is on. A game of checkers before dinner. Stories told in the dark of night. Marshmallows over the fire. Again, the horses whinny and the breeze blows upon me. I feel the blustery snow and hear Aunt Judy belting out carols as we bounce around in the sleigh. I close my eyes and the vision is so clear. The faces, the sights, the sounds and smells of the farmhouse tucked away amidst the rolling hills and endless woods.

As I make my way back up the road, I can hear the voices in joyful chatter as they sit down at that plentiful table together.

—Glenna J.

What would your impressions be if you were asked to jot down descriptive phrases about your home? As I return to Tuckaway Farm in my mind's eye many decades later, I sense a glimpse of nostalgic wonder, and I am filled with gratitude.

Impressions Returning to Tuckaway

Hiding ramshackled in a Wisconsin valley
Secluded, isolated, alone
A declining house, barn, and outhouse
Disheveled, paint-starved, dilapidated
Nurturing a haven of beauty and resources
Apple orchard, berry vines, logging timbers
Nesting high on the hill, a cemetery
Beloved dogs, squirrels, cats, and guinea pigs

Standing in the yard a gigantic oak tree
Climbing, swinging, sitting
Inhabiting surrounding woods
Edible squirrel, rabbit, and deer
Gracing each bush and tree
Cardinals, bluebirds, chickadees
Growing abundantly in hill and valley
Cabbage, Beans, Cucumbers

Celebrating family ties together
Holidays, birthdays, anniversaries
Finding a haven to establish
Roots, tangibility, affirmation
Tucking away for the future
Education, hard work, character, faith, love.

Peering through intervening years
Tranquility, forgiveness, consolation
Pearly white sereneness beckons
Voiceless, soundless, peaceful scene
Trails in fields of harmonious white
Fresh options, new prospects for the future.

While sometimes brutally challenging, winter became my favorite season when I was able to return to Tuckaway Farm with my children. Times spent together sledding, cross-country skiing, and sleigh riding were treasured.

A country winter brings with it great challenges and a need for special preparations to ensure one's safety. The wind lashes across the open acreage whipping up gigantic whirling and swirling snowdrifts.

Memories of a Country Winter

Crocks laden with hand-cut meat
Snow providing the only refrigeration
Cellar replete with summer's produce
Ensuring varied diet and nutrition
Plastic coverings on windows and doors
Rebuffing winter's cold winds
Ropes tied securely to out-buildings
Securing a safe return in blizzards
Batteries by the kitchen wood stove
Guaranteeing energy for vehicles and plow.

10

A Coincidence You Say?

> The world is round and the place which may seem like
> the end may also be the beginning.
>
> —Ivy Baker Priest

It has been said that God paints a beautiful portrait of His goodness upon the canvas of our days. For thirty-seven years, I worked in Minnesota's public schools in various positions in education. Every assignment was my favorite—be it as a classroom teacher, remedial reading teacher, learning disabilities teacher, counselor, in a district administrative position, or as a shared multi-district special education coordinator.

In addition, I had the privilege of establishing a private kindergarten school.

In the 1960s, Minnesota did not mandate school districts to provide kindergarten. Area realtors and a group of parents got together and inquired if I would be willing to create what became known as Progresso-K.

It was a big job to build a school in our basement and have it fire and state approved. I developed the curriculum, taught the students, and did the administrative responsibilities. Gordon did the daily janitorial duties and maintained the playground after his day at work.

After three years of the school's operation, Gordon became critically ill and was not expected to live. Many months later, he was able to return to work; however, it had been necessary for me to have returned to teaching in the public school in the meantime to ensure continuing health benefits and a livable salary for my family.

After retirement, I was introduced to watercolor painting through the Elderhostel (Road Scholar) program. Attending watercolor workshops and art schools became my passion. Every day would find me painting in a little bedroom converted into a studio.

Two years after my husband's death in 2006, I needed to sell my Austin, Minnesota home. The large yard, multiple gardens, and clearing away the winter snows became too physically taxing for me.

The house was only on the market two weeks. The new owner wanted immediate possession but agreed to rent my own house to me for two weeks to allow me time to find housing.

The hunt was on to quickly find a senior condo or townhouse that would allow me to keep my precious little Yorkiepoo. Austin and a half dozen of the surrounding smaller towns, plus Rochester, Minnesota were scoured to no avail. Tomah, Wisconsin was also explored as my daughter resides there. None could be found. Then, Glenna tried to find senior housing on the Internet that would allow a dog. Bingo! Eau Claire, Wisconsin had dozens of possibilities. I purchased a condo and have become active in the association by serving on the board of directors and as a member of the management team.

Ironically, Eau Claire is where I was born nearly eight decades ago. My precious Chase Michael was adopted. I was surprised to learn much later on that his doggie birth certificate listed his place of birth as Eau Claire, Wisconsin also.

The End of the Road

A coincidence you say?

Many years ago, I chose Psalm 32:8 as my life's Bible verse. "I will teach you and instruct you in the way that you shall go. I will guide you with my eye."

The late afternoon of the very day that I signed the closing papers on my condo in July 2008, I met a wonderful man. Jim has become a close friend. He, like my husband, Gordon, has been helpful and supportive of my passion for art.

A coincidence you say?

While I dearly miss my Austin friends and the art community connections there, I am active in two art organizations here in the Chippewa Valley. I have found that warm and loving people abound in any arts group. We are more like family. Multiple venues and opportunities to show one's paintings are ongoing year around, as well as my personal display of my paintings at the local Riverwood gallery on Highway 93 in Eau Claire.

Someone once said, "A bend in the road is not the end of the road, unless you make the wrong turn."

Tuckaway Farm belongs to another person now, but it is only about twenty-six miles from Eau Claire. It seems that in having to relocate to Eau Claire, Wisconsin that I have come full circle.

My Prayer for You

> I pray not that your life will be easy, but that God will use life's difficulties to make you strong in faith and purpose; not that you will be wealthy, but that you will be given abundant resources to give to the needs of others; not that you will be comfortable, but that you will be content in the place and circumstances in which God places you, not that you will be self-sufficient, but that you will learn through your weakness to be totally dependent upon God; not that you will gain status and power over others, but that you will find your deepest fulfillment in being a servant to all.
>
> —Roy Lessin